The Treasure Hunt...

A COMPLETE GUIDE TO INTERVIEWING

Brian P.Carey

Order this book online at www.trafford.com
or email orders@trafford.com

Most Trafford titles are also available at major online book retailers.

Printed in the United States of America.

ISBN: 978-1-4669-7180-6 (sc)

Library of Congress Control Number: 2012922970

Trafford rev. 12/04/2012

www.trafford.com

North America & international
toll-free: 1 888 232 4444 (USA & Canada)
phone: 250 383 6864 ♦ fax: 812 355 4082

DEDICATIONS

To Teresa Carey, my beautiful wife and best friend, you have always believed in my ability to succeed.

To Baby Carey, you are the most important person in my life. You are the reason I consider myself a success now, and I look forward to the day that you are born.

To my parents, Kent and Debby Carey, both of you have taught me the values that I needed to grow into who I am today.

A special thanks to the following people who have supported and believed in my success:

The Cusano Family	*Keith Carey*
The Raymond family	*Lorraine Griffiths*
David Soucy	*Regina Scillitoe*
Josh Davis	*Pamela Jace*
Nathan Hade	*Jack F. Kane*

To the great leaders and authors, whose teachings have made it possible for me to explore who I am and see what I can become:

Jesus Christ	*Zig Zigler*
Benjamin Franklin	*Robert Allen*
Napoleon Hill	*Tom Hopkins*
Brian Tracy	*Gerald Garrity*

To everyone who strives to be a positive influence, both to themselves and to others.

Thank you!

A Note from the Author

All of the information that I have presented within this book has been developed through my personal experience. I was not happy where I was, and needed to make a change for the better.

To start, I realized that if I continued to search for a job in the same conventional way that I was taught, I would keep ending up with the same type of position. Humans are creatures of habit, and I needed to find a different way of looking at things if I wanted to change for the better.

I then began to research various career opportunities. I documented every detail of my research to use as a reference guide. What started out as a journal soon became my own workbook and treasure map to success.

There are many steps that people take for granted throughout the interviewing process. The goal of this book is to bring each of you through these steps with ease, and help you to achieve all of your employment goals. Once you have completed this book you too will have an invaluable reference guide that you will be able to use forever.

My best wishes and blessings,
Brian P. Carey

Take A Step Back To Go Forward

Imagine a child running outside,
Without a care in the land,
Not a sense of time or stress of life,
Just a treasure map in their hand.

It is probably a map that they had made,
To get them through the day.
An adventure laid out, a treasure to find,
Until darkness pulls them away.

But as soon as the sun wakes them up
And breakfast has been swallowed,
The shoes are tied, and the door flung open,
There's a treasure map to be followed.

Now picture yourself chasing your dreams,
But as a little child,
Not a sense of time or stress of life,
Your imagination running wild.

A kid will do what they have to do,
To get to the end of their story,
Digging up their hidden gift,
And basking in the glory.

Take your dreams and see them as real,
Make a map today.
Plan the road to success,
And then be on your way.

Nothing will stop you from hitting your goal,
Once you have it in sight,
Then take the treasure that you have earned,
And sleep peaceful through the night.

By: Brian P. Carey

Table of Contents for:

The Treasure Hunt...
A COMPLETE GUIDE TO INTERVIEWING

The next page is a copy of the treasure map that you will be following on your path to the perfect career. This brain-shaped island represents a blueprint of what you already have within. So collect your tools, follow each step on the map, and uncover the treasure that you deserve.

Treasure Map

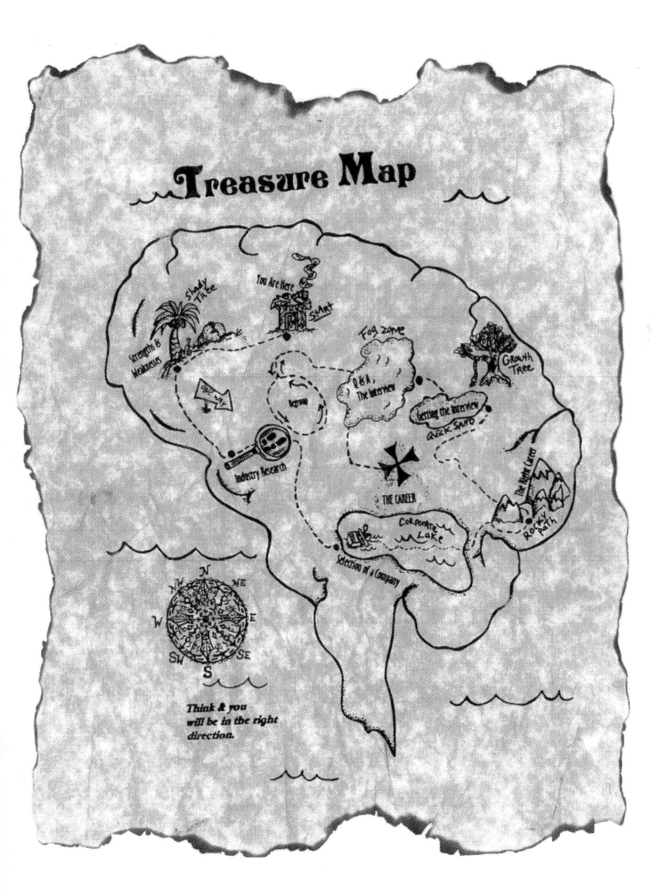

Think & you will be in the right direction.

CLUE#1

The starting point on the map.

Your journey begins here. Until now your life has brought you back to the same place. With this map that you have discovered, your life will be different.
You must first collect the important tools that you will need to be a success.
Good luck!

START

Discovering Yourself Through Goals

"I am finding a career that will contribute to my success."

For every action there is a beginning and an end. Unfortunately, the end results are not always what we want them to be. Due to these circumstances we continue doing what we know, and hope for a lucky break. How is one supposed to change their outcome without seeing a map of their future?

The answer is simple. Make your own map by desiring success, having a goal, making a plan to accomplish your goal, and keeping focused. When you follow these steps consistently, opportunities will begin to appear where you never saw them before.

When a sports team runs onto the field there is desire for a common goal. The goal is to win the game. Each strategy and move has been planned and executed to bring the team to victory. Once the game has been won the team celebrates their accomplishment. They also have their coach to keep them from becoming unfocused. Before the next game the coach will review the strengths and development needs of the entire team, and create a plan for their next win.

With every triumph the team members feel unstoppable. People who once only watched the game soon become fans. The team with the smartest executed plan takes home all of the glory. Eventually they will be known by name as a successful team, and the door of opportunity will open and find them. So how does this example apply to you? How can you become unstoppable?

You are the team that needs a goal to win. Everyone has the ability to develop over time to achieve a desired level of success. Unfortunately not everyone knows or has been taught how to accomplish this task. Criticisms and negative influences often prevent individuals from accomplishing what they truly desire. Use this book as your personal coach, create a plan, and execute it with both the intelligence and passion to win. As a result, confidence, praise, and opportunities will find you.

The following are the steps that you need to be successful in obtaining your goals:

1. *SELECT A GOAL:*

Notice the quote that I typed directly under *Discovering Yourself Through Goals*, at the top of page 2. *"I am finding a career that will contribute to my success."* This statement is written in the present tense.

When I was growing up I would tend to say statements like, "I am going to do this, I will do that, or I want to do it." It sounded great to me at the time, but because I was *going to* do these things there was never a sense of urgency for me to create a plan. Without a plan I never achieved what I wanted. Since I have taught myself how to follow this goal process I have been able to accomplish many things that never seemed possible to me.

Once you state your goal in the present tense you are already participating in the outcome of the goal. If you are already doing something, then you cannot say or think that you will do it later. What if you do not have a goal?

Everyone who achieves success whether it is in the workplace or a relationship has a goal. Pretend that the world is ending in 6 months and there are no limits to what you can have between now and then. What would make you feel like you accomplished everything? Do you want to have a lot of money? Do you want a new home? Perhaps you just want to be happy and improve your way of life.

Within the following spaces make a list of everything that you want to have in life. Do not worry about stating your list in the present tense at the moment. Once you have created your list there will be an outline, beginning on page 4, for you to fill in that will make all of your goals clear and attainable.

For example: *1) Dream Career*

_____	_____
_____	_____
_____	_____
_____	_____
_____	_____
_____	_____

2. *BREAK IT DOWN INTO EASY TO FOLLOW STEPS:*

Once you have completed the list of desired goals use the outline below, and write each of your goals in the order that you wish to accomplish them. For the sake of simplicity, only plan out three to five goals at a time.

Then, write out the steps that you will need to follow in order to complete your goals. In this case the first goal will be to attain your dream career.

To begin, in the space provided next to **A. Goal**, write, *"I am taking the proper steps that I need to find my dream career."* Remember, you want to write each goal within the present tense so that you will be in the process of completing your goal now. It is also important to do the same thing when filling out the steps that you will need to take to accomplish these goals.

Section **A**, numbers **1.**, **2.**, and **3.**, have been filled in to help you. I left enough lines for you to fill out your own steps. If more room is required do not hesitate to use the margins.

A. Goal _____

    1. I am completing all of the exercises within this workbook.

    2. I take the time to focus on how each lesson applies to me.

    3. I remain positive at all times. _____

B. Goal _____

    1. _____
    2. _____
    3. _____
    4. _____
    5. _____

C. Goal _____

    1. _____
    2. _____
    3. _____
    4. _____
    5. _____

D. Goal _____

    1. _____
    2. _____
    3. _____
    4. _____
    5. _____

E. Goal _____

    1. _____
    2. _____
    3. _____
    4. _____
    5. _____

Mark these pages and read them out loud to yourself each day. The more you hear something the more it becomes part of your everyday thoughts. You will begin to notice opportunities that otherwise would have passed you by.

The first car that I ever had was a 1978 Chevy Nova. Before I had a car of my own I use to ride my bike or get a ride from my parents. Once I took possession of my car and made it part of my everyday life I started noticing Chevy Novas everywhere. If you do not have the initial desire to make something important to you then your mind will have no reason to find what you are looking for.

3. *COMPLETE ONE STEP AT A TIME:*

As you begin to see your goal becoming a reality it is very normal to want to jump towards it without finishing what you had planned. Trying to obtain your goal before you are ready is like building a house before the foundation is finished. Everything will collapse and fall apart. Make each step its own separate goal so that you will stay focused, build a strong foundation, and have success on a regular basis.

Each step that you complete within this book will bring you to a new place within your life. As your journey continues you will discover that you have actually completed several small goals. As mentioned within the sports example earlier within this section, the more you win the more unstoppable you will become.

4. *UPDATE YOUR PLAN:*

Life has a unique way of stepping in and creating obstacles for us to overcome throughout our existence. Some people look at these obstacles as dead ends, but the successful person looks at obstacles as a challenge and an experience to grow from.

There is an endless list of speakers and authors that I could quote at this time, but they do not have the content that this section requires. Sometimes the best advice is where you would least expect it. From a film called <u>Better Off Dead</u>, created within the 80's, I quote *"Go down the hill very fast... If something gets in your way, turn!"*

If you are speeding through your goals and something gets in your way, turn! Keep yourself open to all possibilities, modify your plan, and get what you desire. Unplanned circumstances or events may delay the outcome, but ultimately you are the one responsible for getting there.

5. *OBTAIN & MAINTAIN YOUR GOAL:*

The end of your journey should be the beginning of a new journey.

For example:

When you get the career you desire, create another set of goals to keep your job. Read industry books, keep learning about your industry, and come up with creative ways that will make your job easier and more effective. Your new goal will be to set yourself apart from the others by making yourself an asset. Because of this, it is very important that you keep your accomplishment techniques to yourself.

After all, a famous chef within an elite restaurant does not come out of the kitchen and give a recipe card with every entrée. What would be the purpose of going back if you can do it yourself? Follow your recipe to success and keep them coming back for more!

Summary

FORMULA FOR SUCCESS

DESIRE + GOALS + PLANNING = COMPLETED GOALS

COMPLETED GOALS = INCREASED SELF ESTEEM

INCREASED SELF ESTEEM + A DESIRE TO MAINTAIN & COMPLETE MORE GOALS = UNLIMITED POSSIBILITIES

This book focuses on creating a path that will allow you to achieve your career goal. It is up to you to take each step as they come, and enjoy what your own treasure hunt has to offer.

CLUE#2

An analysis of strengths & weaknesses

You now have the tools that you
need, and the right attitude.
Take your treasure map in hand.
It is time to walk into the
shadows. Once there you will
discover what it will take to
continue your journey.

Strength & Weakness Analysis

During interviews strengths and weaknesses are frequently discussed. The interviewer wants to know how you will be an asset to the company. This will be a reference point that will help you with the mindset that you will need to complete the Q&A (Question and Answer) section of this workbook.

Weaknesses

When filling out this section take your time, and be honest with yourself. Your weaknesses don't have to be work related. If you have something that you need to work on, you may want to explore it now.

For example: *1. I don't have much computer experience.*

2. I spend a lot of time on paperwork.

1. _____

2. _____

3. _____

4. _____

5. _____

Weaknesses are never bad to have. They are the keys that will make you successful. Without the knowledge and understanding of what you are weak in, there is no way that you can ever become strong within these areas.

Strengths

How do others see you? How do you see yourself? What qualities will make someone want to hire you?

For example: 1. *I carry my goals on me, and remain focused.*
2. *I work well both as an individual, and within a team environment.*

1. _____
_____

2. _____
_____

3. _____
_____

4. _____
_____

5. _____
_____

Weaknesses to Strengths

Now, take the weaknesses that you came up with on the previous page and change them into strengths.

For example: Weakness = I spend a lot of time on paperwork.

Strength = I am a stickler for detail and understand the value of doing it right the first time, so that I only see it on my desk once.

1. _____
_____
_____
_____
_____

2. _____
   _____
   _____
   _____
   _____

3. _____
   _____
   _____
   _____
   _____

4. _____
   _____
   _____
   _____
   _____

5. _____
   _____
   _____
   _____
   _____

Now you have as much as ten strengths and zero weaknesses. Always look at a weakness as an opportunity to grow. When you interview, what would have been viewed as negative is now a positive.

CLUE#3

The industry research begins here

There is no turning back now.
Your journey is still new, but you
now have twice the strengths to
get you there.
Once you uncover the secret of
the next stop, you will find that
things may not always be as they
seem.

Industry Research

Finding the Right Industry for You!

There are hundreds of businesses and job descriptions available. Even if you already know which industry you want to work in, please take the time to fill out the following section. Things always look different when they are written down. There may be something else that you would like more, but never considered it.

1. Industry/Industries that I want to work in, and why? :

_____

_____

_____

_____

2. Things I enjoy doing (hobbies, games, sports, cooking...):

_____

_____

_____

_____

3. Previous industry experience:

_____

_____

_____

_____

_____

4. Job responsibilities I enjoy doing:

_____

_____

_____

_____

_____

5. Job responsibilities I dislike doing:

_____
_____
_____
_____
_____
_____

Now take all this information that you just wrote down and make a decision. How many of these qualities do you want in a career? Never believe that you can't have work that makes you happy. You can never expect to be happy at work if you don't work to be happy.

Go back and highlight these traits, and when completing your industry research, make sure that the industry has positions available that will allow you to get what you want. If it does not, no matter what others say, explore other options.

Researching Your Industry

Once you have selected an industry you will need to complete research on it. The modern interviewer looks for someone who stands out above the rest. Too many people are out there looking for jobs and not careers. If you go into an interview with detailed knowledge of the industry, and you are able to compare it to both your skills and abilities, it will clearly exhibit your seriousness about the position.

When starting your research, there are many tools to help you. The Internet, books (or magazines), successful people within the industry, and the phone, are all important sources to utilize.

This section has general industry topics for you to fill in. If you use a web-site, book, or company, be sure to write down the source of the information gained (spaces are provided for this purpose starting on page 17). It is important to know the source that helped you. This may also be a question that you have to answer during you interview as well.

Industry Being Researched: *Remember to use the previous exercise results, so that you can select an industry that will make you happy.*

_____

Industry Overview: *Look for information that gives a general description of the industry.*

_____
_____
_____
_____
_____
_____
_____

Things About The Industry That You Like: *Write things that you already knew, and things that you learned. This will be important when asked why you chose this industry.*

_____
_____
_____
_____
_____
_____
_____

Things About the Industry That You Dislike: *Once you have listed any dislikes, try to turn them into a positive like we did for the Strength & Weakness Analysis. If you can not get past the negative points of the industry, then go with your second choice. You may have to do this a few times before you find the right fit for you.*

Negative:

_____
_____
_____
_____

Negative to Positive:

_____

_____

_____

_____

<u>Additional Notes:</u> *If you need to choose another industry you can put your notes within the following space.*

_____

_____

_____

_____

_____

_____

_____

_____

_____

_____

_____

_____

_____

_____

_____

_____

_____

_____

_____

_____

_____

_____

_____

_____

Sources Used For Research

Keeping a record of sources that you use for research is a good habit to possess. Think of it as having your own personalized library. Anytime you need information that pertains to the subject matter at hand you will have a quick reference point. If an interviewer asks what you have read pertaining to the industry you will also be able to produce actual sources. This does a lot for strengthening your credibility on an interview.

<u>Books</u>: *Your local library or bookstores have many resources with the information that you seek.*

_____   _____

_____   _____

_____   _____

_____   _____

_____   _____

<u>Magazines</u>: *Almost every industry has a magazine. The best way to find one is to either go to a business and look at the magazines in the lobby, or call the reception area and ask. Also, look to see if the magazine has an order card in it, or if it has a web-site. While you are there, take any marketing information that has been made available.*

_____   _____

_____   _____

_____   _____

_____   _____

_____   _____

<u>Web-Sites</u>: *Do a general search of the industry. You can also look up a large company's web-site. Often there is an industry overview within the history or business description that is very useful.*

_____   _____

_____   _____

_____   _____

_____   _____

_____   _____

Companies: *When calling a business, ask to speak with someone in marketing, or sales. Tell them that you are doing a research paper, and would like a moment of their time to ask them some questions about their industry. Sales people are famous for liking to talk about what they do, and don't have enough practice doing it, so this might be your most informative angle. Always write down the name of the person that helped you. <u>Do not ask for management</u>. If you end up calling again to ask for an interview, you want to have the knowledge in advance for credibility.*

_____   _____

_____   _____

_____   _____

_____   _____

_____   _____

Any Additional Sources Not Mentioned That You Have Used:

_____   _____

_____   _____

_____   _____

_____   _____

_____   _____

_____   _____

_____   _____

_____   _____

_____   _____

_____   _____

_____   _____

CLUE#4

You have reached Corporate Lake. Selection of a company begins here.

Congratulations!

Many do not make it this far. It takes a lot to realize that you may have been on the wrong path, but I assure you, the correct path is in front of you now.

Be careful on the next step of your journey.

If you try to rush through it, the waters will get rough.

CORPORATE LAKE

Selection of a Company

Making a List

Now that you have chosen an industry, you need to choose what company you would like to work for. Make a list in the following spaces provided of all the companies that you would like to work for. There are 30 spaces. Try to fill out as many as you can. If you already have a newspaper classified, include that company as well.

The purpose of this exercise is to list as many companies that you can think of that would interest you. There is no reason to limit your search to only the classifieds or computer job listings. Some companies don't even advertise for positions that they are looking to fill.

1. _____
2. _____
3. _____
4. _____
5. _____
6. _____
7. _____
8. _____
9. _____
10. _____
11. _____
12. _____
13. _____
14. _____
15. _____
16. _____
17. _____
18. _____
19. _____
20. _____
21. _____
22. _____
23. _____
24. _____
25. _____
26. _____
27. _____
28. _____
29. _____
30. _____

From your list begin by selecting the top 10 companies that interest you, and write them down on page 21 within the spaces provided. Make sure to include each web-site address. Once you locate the web-site for each company print it out completely. This is where you start building your credibility. Companies like to see that you have researched them prior to the interview.

If you do not have access to a computer, consider using the computer at your public library. Most libraries will only charge you for the paper that you use. If you still can't find a computer, call the company itself and ask to speak with a salesperson. No one likes to talk about their company more than someone from the sales department. Remember that their job is very fast paced. It is important to show courtesy by asking if they have time to answer a few questions.

Once the salesperson has answered all of your questions thank them, ask for their full name, and mail them a "Thank You" card. You never know, that salesperson may be your key to get in the door.

Follow up to make sure the person that you spoke with received your card, and while you have them on the phone ask if the company is hiring. Often companies provide their employees with a substantial referral bonus if the person that they referred is hired.

Top 10 Company Choices

Company	Web-Site
1. _____	_____
2. _____	_____
3. _____	_____
4. _____	_____
5. _____	_____
6. _____	_____
7. _____	_____
8. _____	_____
9. _____	_____
10. _____	_____

After reviewing each web-site, or phone discussion, you may find that you do not have an interest in all of your choices after all. For the sake of time management start with the 5 strongest candidates, and fill in the following information starting on page 22.

1. <u>Company Name, Phone Number, & Contact Name:</u>

_____

_____

_____

(a) **Company Description/History:** _List any significant dates or growth in the company. You also want to list the name of the President, VP, and head of the department that you would like to work in._

_____

_____

_____

_____

_____

_____

_____

_____

(b) **What do you like about the company? Why do you want to work there?** _Within this section you will want to list positive traits that will match your job qualifications and strong desires._

_____

_____

_____

_____

(c) **Miscellaneous Information:** _Within the following spaces write down any information that you think will be useful on an interview._

_____

_____

_____

_____

_____

2. Company Name, Phone Number, & Contact Name:

_____

_____

_____

(a) Company Description/History: _List any significant dates or growth in the company. You also want to list the name of the President, VP, and head of the department that you would like to work in._

_____

_____

_____

_____

_____

_____

_____

(b) What do you like about the company? Why do you want to work there? _Within this section you will want to list positive traits that will match your job qualifications and strong desires._

_____

_____

_____

(c) Miscellaneous Information: _Within the following spaces write down any information that you think will be useful on an interview._

_____

_____

_____

_____

3. <u>Company Name, Phone Number, & Contact Name:</u>

_____

_____

_____

(a) Company Description/History: *List any significant dates or growth in the company. You also want to list the name of the President, VP, and head of the department that you would like to work in.*

_____

_____

_____

_____

_____

_____

_____

_____

(b) What do you like about the company? Why do you want to work there? *Within this section you will want to list positive traits that will match your job qualifications and strong desires.*

_____

_____

_____

_____

(c) Miscellaneous Information: *Within the following spaces write down any information that you think will be useful on an interview.*

_____

_____

_____

_____

_____

4. Company Name, Phone Number, & Contact Name:

_____

_____

_____

(a) Company Description/History: _List any significant dates or growth in the company. You also want to list the name of the President, VP, and head of the department that you would like to work in._

_____

_____

_____

_____

_____

_____

_____

_____

(b) What do you like about the company? Why do you want to work there? _Within this section you will want to list positive traits that will match your job qualifications and strong desires._

_____

_____

_____

_____

(c) Miscellaneous Information: _Within the following spaces write down any information that you think will be useful on an interview._

_____

_____

_____

_____

_____

5. <u>Company Name, Phone Number, & Contact Name:</u>

_____
_____
_____

(a) **Company Description/History:** *List any significant dates or growth in the company. You also want to list the name of the President, VP, and head of the department that you would like to work in.*

_____
_____
_____
_____
_____
_____
_____

(b) **What do you like about the company? Why do you want to work there?** *Within this section you will want to list positive traits that will match your job qualifications and strong desires.*

_____
_____
_____
_____

(c) **Miscellaneous Information:** *Within the following spaces write down any information that you think will be useful on an interview.*

_____
_____
_____
_____

The next section will walk you through each step of turning your research into career results!

CLUE#5

Rocky Path is coming up. Choose the right career for you.

Even though it was not easy, you made it through. Be proud of your accomplishments thus far. Now, what do you want to be when you grow up? The path has been laid out for you to follow, and find the answer. Do not let the rough terrain intimidate you.

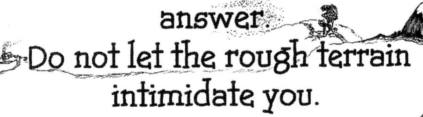

The Right Career

The Position for You!

"What do I want to be when I grow up?"

Make sure that you are looking for a career that you want, and not something similar to what you have had. Habit is comfortable, but not necessarily correct. It is time to free yourself from what you consider to be comfortable within the work place. Forget what you know how to do, and focus on the things that you enjoy doing, or things that you want to learn how to do.

It is OK to follow a dream. Anyone that tells you different probably never followed a dream of their own. Be the one who gets what they want. Wouldn't it be great to look forward to Monday mornings for a change?

Thus far you have set and completed important goals that will contribute to your success. You have been faced with your areas of weakness, and transformed them into valuable skills and qualities. You have also completed valuable research to uncover the industries and companies that will make you happy. Now it is time to select both the salary and position that you will be interviewing for.

Salary Requirements

There is no reason why you should not be compensated for your value as well as your hard work. Even though it has been said, "Money isn't everything" in reality, money pays the bills, and prevents you from losing everything. So, before choosing what career you want, explore what you need to cover your costs and living expenses.

The following exercise will help you to do just that:

Previous or current Salary: $_____

Always set your salary goal higher than what you were or are currently earning. Your goal is to increase your annual earnings. By understanding the value of your previous positions, you will then be able to set a value on your experience/skills.

Monthly Expenses: Determine the total monthly figure. I recommend that you round up on this number to the nearest $100.00 to cover any small forgotten expenses.

Roughly $ _____ Per Month.

How much do I want to save per month? Savings are very important. Even if it is only $10.00 per week, it may seem insignificant now, but within a year you would have saved almost $500.00. It is easy not to plan what we spend, and then we end up with nothing to show for it.

Take the time to plan your savings, and you will have plenty to show for it.

$_____ Per Month.

How much extra money would I like to make? Include the extra amount that you want to make. Movies, hobbies, dating, etc... are all things that cost us extra money. Make this a part of your base desired salary requirements, because it will not be a *Dream Career* if you are living paycheck to paycheck without having fun.

Knowing how much you are worth down to the hour is one of the best motivators when negotiating for the extra money.

For example: If you want to make an extra $5,000.00 per year you would divide that number by the 12 months of the year to get $416.67 per month. To break it down even further, take $416.67 and divide it by the 4 weeks in a month to get $104.17 per week. Then divide $104.17 by the 5 workdays in a week to get $20.83 per day. Finally divide $20.83 by an 8-hour workday to get $2.60 per hour. $2.60 per hour sounds much smaller than asking for $5,000.00.

Desired Salary: Use the following formula to calculate your desired salary.

MONTHLY EXPENSES $_____ + SAVINGS $_____ +

ADDITIONAL PAY (EXTRA) $_____ =

$_____ Desired Salary Per Year

(Divide per year amount by 12) $_____ Desired Salary Per Month

(Divide per month amount by 4) $_____ Desired Salary Per Week

(Divide per week amount by 5 work days) $_____ Per Day,

(Divide per day amount by an 8 hour work day) $_____ Desired Salary Per Hour

If the position will require that you work more than an 8 hour day calculate in the hours that you will be working. The higher the hours the smaller the hourly amount will appear. Smaller numbers are always much easier to negotiate with.

The next exercise will help you discover a great way to link all of your past employment experience together. With a new understanding of your employment history you will be able to successfully demonstrate the path to success that you have been taking all along.

Where Have You Been?

If you are fresh out of school, and do not have a lot of job experience, fill in the experience that you do have. Employers understand that people coming out of school have not had enough time to develop large amounts of experience. This is where internships, after-school jobs, and volunteer work will play a positive role in gaining experience.

The following section should be filled in, starting with your first job. Do not start with your most current position, because the idea of this section is to create a path linking all of your previous jobs to each other in chronological order. I use five, because it does not make a resume too large, and it keeps the interviewer from asking too many questions.

You want to be the one who asks the most questions, because **questions = control**. The interview will be long enough without adding extra facts that may end up distracting the interviewer from realizing the value that you have to offer. Your focus should be on showing that you have plan, asking questions, and listening carefully to the answers.

Complete this section and you will be surprised at what you will be able to say about yourself.

Company #1: _____

Position: _____

From _____ To_____
          Year   *Year*

Job Responsibilities:

- _____
- _____
- _____
- _____
- _____
- _____
- _____

What valuable skill/skills did you develop from this job?

_____
_____
_____
_____
_____

Why did you leave? *Keep this answer simple and positive. No one likes a complainer, no matter how justified they may be.*

_____
_____
_____

Company #2: _____

Position: _____

From _____ To _____
　　　　 Year 　　　 *Year*

Job Responsibilities:

- _____
- _____
- _____
- _____
- _____
- _____
- _____
- _____

What valuable skill/skills did you develop from this job?

_____
_____
_____
_____
_____
_____

Why did you leave? *Keep this answer simple and positive. No one likes a complainer, no matter how justified they may be.*

_____
_____
_____
_____

Company #3: _____

Position: _____

From _____To_____

     Year   *Year*

Job Responsibilities:

- _____
- _____
- _____
- _____
- _____
- _____
- _____
- _____

What valuable skill/skills did you develop from this job?

_____
_____
_____
_____
_____
_____

Why did you leave? *Keep this answer simple and positive. No one likes a complainer, no matter how justified they may be.*

_____
_____
_____
_____

Company #4: _____

Position: _____

From _____ To_____
          Year   *Year*

Job Responsibilities:

- _____
- _____
- _____
- _____
- _____
- _____
- _____
- _____

What valuable skill/skills did you develop from this job?

_____
_____
_____
_____
_____
_____

Why did you leave? *Keep this answer simple and positive. No one likes a complainer, no matter how justified they may be.*

_____
_____
_____
_____

Company #5: _____

Position: _____

From _____ To_____
Year Year

Job Responsibilities:

- _____
- _____
- _____
- _____
- _____
- _____
- _____
- _____

What valuable skill/skills did you develop from this job?

_____
_____
_____
_____
_____

Why did you leave? _Keep this answer simple and positive. No one likes a complainer, no matter how justified they may be._

_____
_____
_____
_____

Now that you know how much money you need to make, and you have listed out a clear career plan, it is time to match all of your requirements with the right job. Where do you find out about available positions?

There are many sources that are available for locating a career. To begin your search, refer to the web site addresses that you listed on page 21. Then read company job descriptions and employee biographies on the Internet to see if your qualifications and values match theirs. Remember to keep an open mind when you begin your search. You may come across a position that is not what you expected, but is exactly what you need.

These are other effective ways to discover what jobs are out there:

- *The Internet*
- *Industry magazines*
- *Newspapers & employment papers*
- *College postings*
- *Staffing companies*
- *Employees within your company selection.*

You now have enough information about the industry, companies, and yourself to get what you want. The next section of the program will show you how to use this information, and move onto the next step in your journey. Congratulations!

*Please use the rest of this page if you have any additional notes or ideas you would like to write down.

_____
_____
_____
_____
_____
_____
_____
_____
_____
_____

CLUE#6

You have reached the Growth Tree. It is time to get the interview.

Knowing where you have been makes it easy to know where you are going.
Move quickly to the next place on the map, but be careful not to get stuck.
If you follow the steps that have been written for you,
The interview will only be a swing away.

Getting the Interview

The steps that you have taken so far have brought you to a very exciting part of your journey. By the end of this section you will know the most effective ways to use the phone, experience letters, and resumes to obtain your interview. You will not only have the skills to get your foot in the door, but you will also have the knowledge to stay there.

The Phone Call

Most help wanted ads request that you do not call. They direct you to either fax or mail your resume. This is a common practice for most large companies. When a position is advertised within the newspaper thousands of people see the posting each day. If the Human Resource Department received a phone call for every inquiry about the position, they would also have to hire an answering service as well to handle the volume. With this in mind it is definitely not a good idea to call the company directly about a posted job. So what do you do?

I am happy that you asked:

1. *Call the general number (you can find it via the Internet, information, yellow pages, etc...).*

2. *Ask for the name and extension of the manager of the department that you are applying for.*

3. *Know what you are going to say in advance (practice).*

4. *PLAY DUMB! Inform them that you have researched their company and industry on your own, and would like a chance to stop in for a visit to discuss how you can benefit their company when they start hiring.*

   This method is very effective because:

   (a) You completely skip over the human resource pile.

(a) Companies usually have an employee referral program, and you are speaking with an employee.

(b) There is something to be said for the innocent. Which do you think is more appealing to a company, someone who called because they saw an ad, or someone who called because of a true interest in the company?

1. Be prepared if they say to fax your resume to human resources. If this happens you may want to say: " I will actually be in the area tomorrow morning. I can drop it off in person. Will you be there?" This will often result in your first interview.

Most of the time using this method works. I used step five on one phone call, and the manager set an appointment with me. During our conversation I found out that the position was over two hours from my house. Unfortunately I had to decline.

However, the manager was impressed with my knowledge of the industry, and asked me if I wanted to interview at an office closer to my house. He even went one step further and said that he would fax my resume personally to his colleague, and follow up with a phone call.

If I faxed my resume to the number in the paper I never would have had this opportunity. Not only did I avoid wasting my time, I was also able to have my resume handed directly to the hiring party. Have fun with this method. You have nothing to lose and everything to gain!

Before making the first call practice what you are going to say. Nothing sounds worse to a prospective employer than someone who is having trouble getting his or her point across. Chances are you have never had to practice a telephone call before, so what is the most effective method to practice?

The best way to do this is to record yourself asking for the interview. Tape recorders are inexpensive, and are worth their weight in gold. No one is as critical as you are. If you sound good to yourself, then most likely you will sound good to others. If you do not sound so good, then recording your voice will give you a chance to practice until it is right. Where else will you get the chance in life to rewind something that you should have said differently?

When The Call Is Not Enough

Let's say that you call and get the manager's voicemail, or they tell you once again to fax in your resume. First of all, if you do get their voicemail do not leave a message. If you leave a message before you meet with them you can count on being one of their many deletes of the day. No one wants to bother with someone they do not know, especially if they have a full schedule of important calls and projects to complete.

In a case where the department head insists that you send your resume to human resources, hope is not lost, and neither is your time. With this in mind *I do recommend faxing or e-mailing a letter-of-experience.* A letter-of-experience should mirror all of the key words and phrases that are within the job description. Make sure that you complete the heading as you would on your resume (refer to the example on page 42).This gives your letter the appearance of a cover letter, and is an easy way to keep your entry different from the rest of the resumes.

In most cases, the person who is reviewing the resumes will see your letter with the dominant company key words and phrases, and put it in the "Possible" pile. Remember these are people too. Sorting through countless numbers of resumes is a boring thing to do, and the easier you make it the better chance you will have getting the interview. What else can you do to make sure you're your letter has been seen by the proper person?

Although it may seem unconventional, send a "Thank You" card with a hard copy of your letter in it. If your first letter, for whatever reason, made its way into the trash do not worry. If you send a "Thank You" card it will most likely be passed on to the department that sets up the interviews. Having a copy of your experience letter within the card will give you a second chance to obtain your interview.

Another way to ensure that your letter has been placed in the right hand is to *send a "Thank You" card to the head of the department that you will be interviewing with.* Chances are you have already spoken with them, and they sent you to human resources. This does not mean that you should not send a thank you card to the person that you spoke with. Their time is valuable, and they were nice enough to direct you to the proper person.

Go ahead and put your experience letter within the "Thank You" card for the department head. Let them know in the card that you appreciate the time that they spent with you on the phone, and that you have included a copy of the letter that you have sent human resources, and look forward to meeting with them. You have now sent your letter three times.

If you did not get the chance to speak with the head of the department, then you should not send them a card or your letter-of-experience.

As long as you work smart you will not have to spend all of your time searching for a job. You will have to spend your time researching, interviewing, and following up. If you follow these steps, you will have a much stronger chance of securing that first meeting.

Developing Your Experience Letter

Developing the experience letter is very easy. The following section of this program displays a job description, and an example of how to set up your letter. Refer to "Where Have You Been" starting on page 30 of this book. Can you link both your past and current experience to what the description is asking for? If you can there is no reason why you can't get an interview.

The job description lists for you what is most important to the company. When writing your letter, use the words and phrases in the order that they appear within the job description. It seems too easy, but I assure you it is very effective. If these qualities were not required for the position then they would not be listed.

Example of Job Description

Job Description for the 123 company: The 123 company is an established supplier of 123 super components. We are currently looking to expand our sales team. The perfect candidate will be both self-motivated and organized within a fast-paced environment. They will possess leadership ability, and be able to handle a multi-task team focused environment.

From this example I will extract the important words and phrases so that you will see just how easy it is to write your letter (page 42).

Self-Motivated,	*Organized,*	*"Within a fast-paced environment,"*
Leadership Ability,	*Multi-Task,*	*Team Focused,*

Notice the content within the example letter. The letter mirrors exactly what the company is looking for. For demonstration purposes I have underlined each of the words and phrases that I used.

EXAMPLE LETTER:

MARY SMITH

Street   Home Phone
City,State,& Zip code   Work Phone

Receivers Name
Occupation
Address

Dear Receivers Name,

On (date) I had the opportunity to speak with, (Department head or person that you spoke to about the position) and they recommended that I get in touch with you.

Based on my previous positions, I have successfully completed all of my goals by being both self-motivated and organized. I found it necessary to plan out my day the previous evening so that I did not lose focus within the fast-paced environment that I have been accustom to working in.

On several occasions I have also received recognition for demonstrating leadership qualities within a multi-task team focused environment.

I appreciate your consideration, and look forward to the opportunity of delivering my resume in person.

Thank you for your time,

Mary Smith
Mary Smith

It is now your turn. Select your number one career choice and complete your own experience letter.

YOUR LETTER-OF-EXPERIENCE:

Company: _____

Job Description:

_____
_____
_____
_____

Letter of Experience:

_____
_____
_____
_____
_____
_____
_____
_____
_____
_____

Do not feel that because you did not send a resume you will be overlooked. The idea of the letter-of-experience is to keep the reviewing process simple, and let the company know that you possess all of the qualities that they are looking for. Work smart, and skip the extra work. Businesses appreciate and respect people who think, and work efficiently.

Notice the last sentence of the example on page 42. It is very important to mention that you look forward to the opportunity of delivering your resume in person. This shows that you not only have the qualities that they are looking for, but you will also take the time to hand deliver your resume when they need it.

When you have successfully completed all of your telephone calls, sent out your letters-of-experience, and "Thank You" cards, there is no good reason why you should not get offered an interview.

When you accept the interview make sure that you ask what time will be best for them. If you are currently employed and can't get any time off for an interview, let the interviewer know. They will appreciate your integrity, and try to work with you. Never take an unplanned day off with your current position. No one will respect this decision. It is a small world, and more times than not it will catch up to you. Suggest that you can meet with them before their day begins, or at the end of the day on their way home. Offer a Saturday morning if you think that they are weekend workers. A coffee doesn't hurt either.

Be prepared to be flexible if a company calls you requesting that a resume be sent. Send the resume with a "Thank You" card, and know that someone must have liked what your letter contained if they made the effort to call you.

What should your resume contain?

The Resume

First of all, the days of writing only one resume with a cover letter are over. Everyone uses them, and most of them look the same when sitting on the human resource desk. I know people that have sent out over 75 resumes at once, and all they have received for their time is a generic note card thanking them for their application.

In most cases these people received generic cards, because they sent out generic resumes. Each resume that you send should be created specifically for both the company and position for which you are applying. Would you rather get a holiday card that has your name on it with a personal message, or would a card that says "Hey you, happy holidays" be OK? How do you both customize your resume and make it stand out? How can you avoid wasting your valuable time?

The resume does not have to be as difficult as one might think. From using the process that I have developed, the resume will not be the key that gets you in the door. In most cases, it will be a one-page outline and guide that you will be using on your interview once you are already in the door.

The style of the resume changes on a regular basis, however the content will always remain the same. In order to keep this book timeless, content will be our area of focus. Current styles can be found in updated resume books or services that specialize in the latest eye catching formats.

The next step in writing a successful resume is getting your information organized and placed in an easy to follow outline. Do not be intimidated by writing your outline. For simplicity sake, try to imagine the order of your resume like ordering food in a restaurant.

I.   *Resume*   = *The restaurant*

      A. *Objective* = *The menu*

      B. *Education* = *The appetizer*

      C. *Work Experience/Work History* = *The entrée*

      D. *Awards & Honors* = *The dessert*

Each one of the positions that you found should have a job description. Some will be more detailed than others. Look at similar jobs, and see what their descriptions are as well. Once you have them you will have what it takes to write an effective objective within your resume.

A. Objective: In my opinion this is the most important section within your resume. The content is very crucial as well, but I am sure that you will agree, without an attractive objective (menu), there will be no reason for the reader to continue.

You always want this section to be short and to the point. Your objective should focus only on <u>how you can benefit their company</u>. Take key words directly from the job descriptions that you have found.

Example: **<u>Job Description:</u>** *Manager- The perfect candidate will have a 4 year degree in business, and demonstrate a take-charge leadership attitude, with the ability to handle a multi-task environment at a fast pace.*

What are the benefits that you can provide for the company? If you have a degree, you demonstrate a take-charge leadership attitude, and your able to handle a multi-task environment at a fast pace.

Notice the job description began with "The perfect candidate." This should tell you only one thing. If you want to be the perfect candidate, then you need to take what they give you and introduce yourself as the perfect candidate.

For example:

OBJECTIVE:

To establish a management career within a multi-task, fast paced environment, where I will be able to utilize my business degree and take-charge leadership attitude to ultimately contribute to the company's over all profit.

It is your turn. Use the career that you selected as your number one choice on page 41 for this resume. For all additional positions please refer to the back of the book where I have included several blank resume outlines for you to complete.

Company: _____

Position: _____

OBJECTIVE:

_____
_____
_____
_____
_____

Now that you have successfully written your objective as a benefit for the company, there is a reason for the reader to keep reading. You have got them hungry, now it is time to bring out the appetizer.

The appetizer is meant to satisfy the initial hunger. I like to do this by listing my education. By placing the education portion of your resume first, you are positioning the reader to want to learn more about you. To keep within the parameters of the food example, you are giving them a taste of things to come. Once the reader sees what you have done to prepare for the workforce, it will be time to bring in the experience (entrée).

The only exception for this rule would be if the job description lists that the experience is more important. In this case you would list your experience then your education.

Let's begin with the content of the education section:

B. Education: This section should be simple. You only want to list your degree or certificate, the school that was attended, the year of completion, and the address.

Also make a list of field related work programs and activities that will enhance your self-image. When including these qualifications remember to adjust your key words and phrases to match each company.

Your entry should appear similar to this:

EDUCATION:

B.A. BUSINESS MANAGEMENT, *Hearuwento College,   Graduated (year)*
Somewherein, MA
- *Received high academic honors.*
- *Attended several seminars relating to my field of study.*
- *Participated in work-study program for 4 years.*
- *Interned for 2 semesters within XYZ Company.*

All of the bulleted sentences are brief, and leave room for further discussion. Because of this, I do not list what honors were received, which seminars were attended, what work-study positions were held, or what was accomplished during the internship program. This will allow the interviewer the chance to ask you to expand upon these.

Now complete your EDUCATION portion of your resume. If you have more than one school to list I have included two sections for you to fill in. All of the spaces that are provided for you on the next page do not have to be completed. Three or four descriptions will be plenty to get the reader motivated to continue.

EDUCATION:

1. _____, _____ _____
       Name of School   *Town/City, State*   *Year of Completion*

- _____
- _____
- _____
- _____
- _____
- _____

2. _____, _____ _____
       Name of School   *Town/City, State*   *Year of Completion*

- _____
- _____
- _____
- _____
- _____
- _____

Keeping in the spirit of this exercise, it is time to bring in the entrée. The experience section of your resume is the substance of your application. This is the main part of your resume where you can give the receiving party everything that they are looking for.

C. Experience: Now that you have finished listing your education, it is time to bring out the main course, the EXPERIENCE. This has to be completed with great care. Up until this point you have followed a pattern that has made the reader want to keep on reading. This is where you want to show progression within the workforce, and how it will benefit the company that you are interviewing with. How will you do this? Easy, support your objective with facts.

Again, refer back to the "Where Have You Been" portion of this program starting on page 30. Within this section you were instructed to list your previous positions, skills, and experience. Once all the information was filled in, you were able to tie it all together to demonstrate an actual career path.

The good news is you already have this part of your resume complete. All you have to do is match each skill with key words that fit the job that you seek. Most of the words that you will use will be directly from the job description. However, you do not want to confine yourself to only the job description. Eventually you will end up repeating yourself. So, where can you get additional key word and phrases that will help you while writing your resume?

Use the pages from the web-site that you printed for a previous exercise on page 20. Make sure that you have printed the home page, biographies, history of the company, and any employment information.

Then, underline or highlight all the key words that make up what the company truly stands for (their goals and corporate vision). Bring this highlighted web-site with when you go on your interview. When asked why you should be the one to be hired, you can take out their web- site and show them how much you have in common with their company. This is always an impressive tool to have.

For example:

*The company that you are interviewing with has a section within their web site that mentions they are a **team-oriented group** of people. The focus of their business is to **make the customer happy**, and deliver a **quality product** that their **representatives stand behind 100%.***

*The job description states that the hiring company is looking for a **numbers focused individual**, with the ability to grow into a **leadership** position.*

Given this information, your entry may look similar to this:

EXPERIENCE:

ACCOUNT EXECUTIVE, XYZ Company, Somewhere, MA   2000-Present

- _Organized weekly team meetings focused on customer retention._
- _Delivered a quality product to my customers, which supported my 60% closing average._
- _Established an effective training program that increased company sales 20% from last year._

Notice that each bulleted sentence focuses on what the interviewer will be looking for. This is where you want to be specific. If it is a numbers focused company, then give numbers. If they are looking for leadership qualities, then show how you have successfully taken the initiative to improve the company that you represent.

Do not change what you did on the job. Make sure that your descriptions are honest, but also represent all of the qualities that the interviewer will be looking for.

From "The Right Career For You" section you completed five job and skill descriptions. Using your experience starting on page 30, combined with the format that we just reviewed (using key words and phrases), fill out the following EXPERIENCE section starting with your most current job.

The next exercise uses the same career choice that you used when completing your objective:

EXPERIENCE:

1. _____, _____   _____-_____
       Position/Title   _Company Name_   _Years Employed_

_____
          Town/City, State

- _____
- _____
- _____
- _____
- _____
- _____

2. _____, _____   _____-_____
      Position/Title   *Company Name*   *Years Employed*

_____
      Town/City, State

- _____
- _____
- _____
- _____
- _____
- _____

3. _____, _____   _____-_____
      Position/Title   *Company Name*   *Years Employed*

_____
      Town/City, State

- _____
- _____
- _____
- _____
- _____
- _____

4. _____, _____   _____-_____
Position/Title   *Company Name*   *Years Employed*

_____
Town/City, State

- _____
- _____
- _____
- _____
- _____
- _____

5. _____, _____   _____-_____
Position/Title   *Company Name*   *Years Employed*

_____
Town/City, State

- _____
- _____
- _____
- _____
- _____
- _____

Your resume is almost finished. Your objective states how you are a benefit to the company; the education portion of your resume demonstrates the degree of your preparation; and your experience paints a clear picture of your career path towards the company that you have selected. So, why do you need an Awards and Honors section?

D. Awards & Honors: The interviewer is always looking for well-rounded candidates who will be able to represent the company environment. Everything that you include in your list that demonstrates the company environment will be "Icing on your cake." Even if you do not have the space on your resume, it is important that you make the space to include this section.

Are you ready for dessert? While completing this portion of your resume, make sure that you include key words and phrases from the company. It is also necessary to list your awards and honors in an order that will support your career path.

AWARDS & HONORS:

- _____
- _____
- _____
- _____
- _____
- _____
- _____

The next section will show you how to prepare for the interview so that you get asked to come back. As long as you remain focused and go after what you want, getting the second interview will not be difficult. Have fun and be creative.

CLUE#7

Practicing the Questions and Answers will take you to the next clue.

Your journey has taken you to many new places.
Leaving your place of comfort, picking up valuable tools along the way, and crossing over various obstacles have prepared you for the next step.
Here you will practice your strategy for the interview, and find clarity.

General Interview/Q&A's & Theory

Before Your Interview

Congratulations! You have completed almost all of the steps within your Treasure Hunt. You are prepared and ready to get the career that you deserve. Do not be intimidated by the interviewer. In the interview you will determine if the company is good enough for you. The research has been done, and you know what you are looking for in a company. So, how are you going to present yourself on the interview?

Before I deliver a presentation, speak in public, or interview, there are four specific areas that I like to focus on. They have a positive impact on both my confidence and self-esteem 100% of the time. These areas include practicing outloud, relaxing, visualizing, and dressing to impress.

Practice, practice, and just when you think that you have it, practice it again. It is a fact that the more you practice the better you get. Unfortunately, interviewing is a one shot performance, and there is not a lot of opportunity to review technique. That is why you have to create the opportunity.

As I mentioned on page 39, a tape recorder is a sound investment. Where else can you hear how you sound. If you sound uncomfortable to yourself, then others will also see you as uncomfortable.

I record myself asking an interview question, pause, and then answer it. If my answer sounds bad when I play it back, I rewind it to the end of the question, and answer it all over again. Sometimes I do this five or six times before I like how it sounds. That is five or six interviews that I did not lose by being prepared.

Keep on recording yourself until you have gone through all aspects of an interview. Use the questions and answers that I have prepared for you within this section as your guide. When you are finished, play the entire interview back, and hear how good it sounds. Hear how good you sound, take a deep breath, and relax.

Relaxing plays an important role in obtaining your dream career. Being able to control your levels of enthusiasm is a very important skill to possess. When you are relaxed it is easier to focus on your goals and get what you want. In this case a job offer was made. Unfortunately we live in the "Real World" where there never seems to be enough time to get anything done. So, how do you find the time to relax?

Start by looking at your day. No one takes up every waking moment with work. There are time wasters all around us. The TV, the radio, colleagues that want to "talk" about work, and coffee breaks, are only a few distractions and time wasters that can be trimmed down. Don't get rid of them all at once. Start by putting down the remote control for thirty minutes, and isolate yourself from everyone and everything.

Once you are alone, close your eyes, take a deep breath, and clear your mind of all thoughts that keep you running around all day and even while you sleep. I like to picture my problems and daily tasks as objects that I can put in a big box and access them when I am done.

The mind works hard all of the time, and it needs rest. The better you are to your mind the better it will be to you. By concentrating only on how your body fits in with the air around you, the world will all of a sudden slow down, and piece by piece your purpose will begin to define itself to you.

Without going too far off the planet, I am simply trying to state the obvious. A dog will chase its tail in circles until it gets dizzy and falls down. You are not a dog. You are a thinking human being that needs to stop chasing your tail. The world moves a lot less when you stop and really see what is there. Be good to yourself and invest some time in relaxing.

Once you have found yourself calm and in control, visualize the actual interview. Picture yourself walking into the room. Introduce yourself while extending your hand to greet the interviewer. Now see them offering you a seat. Go through the entire process within your mind as if you were really there. Enjoy the fresh smell of the coffee, hear all of the background noises from the office, and feel the warmth of the sun radiating from the huge picture window that you are sitting next to. Go through all of the steps in great detail, and ask for the job. The more you practice the easier it will be when you go on your real interview. If you believe and clearly picture something happening enough times it eventually will.

You have practiced your interviewing out-loud, and you have imagined yourself getting through the interview successfully. How will you present yourself? How will you show the interviewer that you mean business?

Dress as if you were being sworn in as President of the United States. Once you get the job, let your employer tell you what the proper attire is. Do not guess what the company's dress code is.

You are much better off overdressing than under dressing. The interviewer will respect you for your effort, and you will feel great, because you will look great.

You will also have established a positive image in the mind of the interviewer. A solid first impression will give you their undivided attention. A bad first impression means that, short of standing on your head, and juggling flaming coconuts, impressing the interviewer will be difficult if not impossible. Now get ready to shake hands, introduce yourself, and sell the entire package called You.

Selling Yourself

How can you sell yourself if you are not a salesperson? Selling is something that we all do without even knowing it. People talk about things that either upset or excite them. Everything else is not worth discussing, because there is no benefit in talking about something that doesn't mean anything to you. In most cases, the more extreme the situation, the more one will want to tell someone about their experience.

Have you ever been out to a restaurant, and had a great meal, or perhaps you also saw a movie that night, and it was horrible? What do you do the next time a friend calls, and asks how you have been?

Chances are you will tell them how great your meal was, and how horrible the movie was. These conversations usually begin with "You have to try the ...., it was delicious. "It just melted in my mouth" or, "Don't waist your money on ..., it was long, and dragged out, with no plot." The next time your friend is goes out, they will probably go to the restaurant, but avoid the movie.

Passion promotes action. If you truly believe that something has value, and there is nothing better, others will feel your enthusiasm, and see the value as well. So far you have learned how to set goals, and establish a plan to get what you want; you have discovered up to ten strengths that you did not know you possessed; and you have also defined the industry, company/companies, and position that will make you happy. If you are capable of getting excited about food or a movie, then you should be ecstatic about yourself.

Imagine how you would want someone to describe you if there was a million dollars riding on the outcome of their description. Hear the words within your mind, and repeat them until it comes easy to you. Now take this positive attitude on your interview, and get someone to feel what you are feeling. This will increase your value both in the interviewer's eyes and your own as well.

Q&A & Theory

You have earned your interview. Again, forget about the traditional way of thinking. You are at this point because you were looking for a career that would be a great match for both yourself and the company that you are interviewing with.

If you have followed this program completely to this point, there is no need for you to be nervous. The awkward feeling of uncertainty is no longer an issue. You already know that your qualifications match the position or you would not be there. You also know that you have a plan, which puts you on the same playing ground as the interviewer.

Before walking into the office and sitting down in front of your potential new employer, you must be prepared. There are several questions that companies like to ask each person that is interviewing. These questions are designed to probe and discover what is beyond the resume. After all, on an interview, personalities need to match as well as skills and qualities. So how do you make sure that your personality comes across without complications?

Much like the game of poker, you don't want to show all of your cards, but you want to keep in control without coming off as a "bluffer". Nothing kills a first impression more than too much information too fast. It demonstrates insecurity, a lack of control, and poor planning skills. The best way to remain the one who is guiding the interview process, is to listen. As Brian Tracy, a world famous motivational speaker, stated at a seminar that I attended, "There is a reason that you only have one mouth, but two ears."

Always listen completely, and pause before each answer. I call this the "Silent Umm...". This shows the interviewer that you respect them by making sure that they are finished with their thoughts. It also reinforces that you are paying close attention to details. No one likes someone who is constantly waiting to speak. It leads one to believe that the person who is "listening" is more interested in their own agenda rather than the content of the conversation. You may think that you look smart by answering the question quickly, but in actuality, you come off as obnoxious.

After you pause and make sure that it is a proper time to respond, be complete with your answers, and always ask questions. No matter where you are, or what situation you find yourself in, **questions = control.**

The next section lists several of the most commonly asked questions on an interview for any career choice. Remember to keep an open mind, and always picture yourself answering these questions. Practice out loud once you have your own answers (use a tape recorder) so that it will come out natural and not rehearsed.

This section has been written in the following format to simplify the questioning portion of the interview:

QUESTION #: *The question that may be asked by the interviewer is typed out in bold letters.*

EXPLANATION: *Each question that is asked has a hidden agenda. This will uncover the meaning of each question for you.*

SUGGESTON: *Based on the explanation, I recommend how to answer so that the interviewer will see a connection between you and their company.*

NOW YOU TRY: *You may interview with a variety of companies, so come up with your own answer that you can use comfortably for any job that you are applying for. If my format flows evenly for you, then feel free to use it.*

QUESTION #1: *Why do you want to work here?*

EXPLANATION: The interviewer does not want to hear generic answers like: "I have always wanted to work here"; "I am looking for a job and saw your ad in the paper"; or "This is my dream job." They are looking for specific reasons to hire you.

SUGGESTION: Be specific when answering this question. If you know the mission statement or company description from your research, use them. If you can work these same goals and ideals into your answer they will come across as benefits that you will provide.

If the company sells a particular product or service, make sure that you have researched it thoroughly. Your answer may sound something like this:

I want to work for a company that loves (name of product or service) as much as I do. Based on all the research that I have done on your company, I know that we are an effective match because…(this is were you match two or three of you qualities to the company. What is it about the company that brings you here each morning?

By asking this question the interviewer has no choice but to answer, and prevents an immediate follow-up question. The prospective employer will share with you the values that are important to them personally. Pay close attention to their answer. You will be able to customize your presentation based on what is said.

NOW YOU TRY:

_____
_____
_____
_____
_____
_____
_____

QUESTION #2: *What do you consider to be your strongest asset, and why? This question may also be worded as, What is you greatest strength?*

EXPLANATION: The prospective employer simply wants to see if your greatest asset matches what they need.

SUGGESTON: Within the job description, the first quality requirement is usually the most important. Look for phrases like, "The perfect candidate must....", "To be considered, the candidate must...".Based on this your answer should be that simple.

For example:

Job Description: The perfect candidate must possess strong leadership qualities.

My strongest asset is that I possess leadership qualities. I have demonstrated them not only in my previous employment, but .... (you want to isolate specific examples where you successfully applied your leadership qualities). What do you feel is the most important quality for this position?

Pay attention to their answer. Chances are the interviewer will confirm that what you said contains the qualities that the company is looking for. Confirmation of your answer is very important, and it demonstrates that you are on the same page. If they do not have the same answer, at least you still have time to work it into your interview.

NOW YOU TRY:

_____
_____
_____
_____
_____
_____
_____
_____

QUESTION #3: *What are your weaknesses? Explain.*

EXPLANATION: Obviously the interviewer wants to see what may prevent you from doing your job.

SUGGESTON: Depending on the position each weakness should vary. Refer back to pages 10-11 under Weakness to Strengths. If you did not answer exactly what the interviewer wanted to hear within your strength answer, this is the section to do it.

One weakness may be that you are interviewing for a position that requires the use of computers, and you do not have a lot of experience with different programs. After you asked what their important qualities were, the interviewer's definition of leadership qualities may have been the ability to adapt, and this may have not come out when you answered about your strengths.

A strong response for this may be:

I know that this position requires the use of various computer programs, and I do not have experience in all of them. I do know that I have used (list the programs that you have experience using), and it only took me a short time to adapt to the language of each program. I like to buy books on things that I do not know so that I can make my work more efficient. What programs do you use here that I will need to learn before starting?

By stating this weakness, I have put myself back into the spotlight, and removed the possibility of creating a negative image of myself. By asking what programs I will need to learn BEFORE starting, the employer knows that there will be less training to be done. Less training means a quicker return on their investment.

NOW YOU TRY:

_____
_____
_____
_____
_____
_____

QUESTION #4: *What do you do to relax, hobbies...?*

EXPLANATION: Companies are aware that people have families, and hobbies. They don't necessarily want to know that you like to knit as much as they want to know that you can provide stability within your performance. This is why most companies prefer well-rounded individuals. Prospective employers look for both direction and focus. They want to know that they are not hiring a burnout.

SUGGESTON: Answer this question with pride. No one likes to see that someone spends their time on things that they do not enjoy or enjoy talking about. If you do not show enthusiasm about you personal life then what positive value can you possibly bring to work?

No self pride = No self worth =
No enthusiasm or fuel to go on = BURNOUT

Within your answer also demonstrate that you have the ability to relax. Many people want to relax, but end up worrying, and bringing undesired stress to their life instead.

Uncontrollable stress = No direction = BURNOUT

One of the best ways to answer this question is:

I can control and direct my levels of enthusiasm and motivation at will, which allows me to relax when I need to. Whether it's spending quality time with my family, (state two or three hobbies), or reading industry related literature to keep myself updated, this ability helps to maintain a strong balance between both my work and home environments.

This will demonstrate the enthusiasm, direction and focus that they are looking for. It always amazes me how the easily overlooked questions can have the strongest impact on whether or not you are hired.

NOW YOU TRY:

_____

_____

_____

_____

_____

_____

QUESTION #5: *Where do you see yourself five years from now?*

EXPLANATION: The interviewer wants to hear that someone is not a job jumper. They do not want to be used as a stepping stone for someone's career path.

The answer "I want to advance in this company, and be here," is a common phrase that won't get you too many points. The key is to be different, and to set you apart from all the others.

SUGGESTON: The person who answers this question with great care, with an understanding of the company's needs, will be the person who successfully moves to the next question.

Here is an example of an effective way to handle this question:

I am the type of person who believes in my goals to the point where I have them written down where I can read them twice per day. One of my goals is that I have a career that I can take pride in by (use key words and phrases from the job description, mission statement, and/or company history). Where do you see this company, in these regards, five years from now?

With this question asked, you will want to **pay attention to every detail of the answer.** The interviewer will be telling you exactly where the company is going, where it has been, and what their role will be in getting it there. Just by asking where the company will be in five years, you will be giving yourself the best present for anyone who has ever sat in the interview hot seat.

NOW YOU TRY:

_____
_____
_____
_____
_____
_____
_____
_____
_____

QUESTION #6: *What did you dislike about your last position/manager?*

EXPLANATION: This is very much like the "Weakness" question. The interviewer wants to see how negative you can be. There are no perfect jobs, and there are no perfect managers. If you left your last job for negative reasons, even if it was due to poor management, it will be a strong indicator that you may not be responsible.

Successful employees take responsibility for the outcome of any situation. The responsible can turn a negative into a positive by working with what they have to get the job done. The interviewer wants to see if you can make lemonade with a lemon.

SUGGESTON: This question should be answered very carefully. It is easy to say negative things about something that you are leaving, or someone that you did not like working for. You will want to set up your answer by doing the following in advance:

The Position:

What did not like about you previous position? Honestly answer this question.

Example: **The hours were long, I was not getting paid enough for the work I was doing.**

NOW YOU TRY:

_____

_____

_____

Now turn your gripe into something positive:

Example: I don't have anything negative to say about my last job. The position taught me patience, and reinforces my ability to work with a wide variety of personalities. Unfortunately there was no room for growth. I decided it was time to take my developed skills, and position myself within a company where I will be able to grow and be part of a team.

NOW YOU TRY:

_____

_____

_____

_____

_____

The Manager:

Treat this the same way. First write out what you did not like about your previous boss.

Example: **My manager was never available, and would come out once a week to yell at everyone for not doing everything how he wanted it. Then he/she would disappear for another week. It was very stressful.**

NOW YOU TRY:

_____

_____

_____

_____

_____

Now turn your gripe into something positive:

Example: **I can't say anything bad about my last manager. He/She was very good at administrative work. I never saw him/her often, which gave me the opportunity to show both initiative and responsibility. I was always able to finish my projects on time, and my boss was always available to give constructive criticism or praise.**

NOW YOU TRY:

_____

_____

_____

_____

_____

Even though you were asked to say something bad about your previous position/manager, you do not have to give a negative answer. If you just saw a movie that was great, and your friend asked if it was bad, you would say that the movie was great.

This would help your friend decide whether or not to go see the movie. The interview question being asked is the same as the movie example. You want to make the interviewer believe that no matter what the situation, you will remain focused with a positive attitude at all times.

QUESTION #7: *What do you know about our company, product, or services?*

EXPLANATION: An interviewer will ask this question for several reasons. They are looking to see your level of motivation, commitment and enthusiasm; they want to see what levels of training you will require; and the interviewer wants to see if you are honest.

SUGGESTON: Do not pretend to know answers if you don't. You will be asked for details, and if you do not have any, the interview will be over. Don't be afraid to say that you don't know.

Based on knowing a little bit about the company, product, or service, in most cases, this is the best way to handle this answer:

I have a general understanding of what your company offers from what I have read on the Internet (or any other source that you may have used). What type of training does your company provide on this subject matter, and is there anything that I will be able to take home to read on my time?

When you answer their question in this manner, you are demonstrating motivation, commitment, and enthusiasm. It also shows that you will not be difficult to train, because you are the type of person that likes to do what it takes to learn even if it is not during work hours. This is seen as an asset to most companies (try writing your answer in the space provided on the next page).

NOW YOU TRY:

_____

_____

_____

_____

_____

_____

_____

QUESTION #8: *There are several other candidates just as qualified as yourself, what can you bring to the table that others can not?*

EXPLANATION: By asking this question the interviewer is looking for something that makes you stand out.

SUGGESTON: The other candidates are qualified, experienced, and have a desire for employment. When asked this question most candidates like to restate their strengths, and/or how they will benefit the company. This is a good way to repeat your positive traits, and keep yourself on the top of their list.

However, for the sake of getting more out of the question, and making your answer the cement that gets you the position, you should take your answer a step further. Go ahead and repeat, but don't stop there:

My understanding is that to be considered for this position one must (fill this in with several traits from the job description, strengths, skills, experience...). I am sure that several other candidates represent these qualities. However, I not only have the ability to set and execute my goals, I also take great pride in my ability to truly listen. By this I mean, many people only hear what is said. I don't only hear words, but I hear tones, styles, wants, and needs. I believe that listening is the root of developing respect. Do you also feel that this is a very important trait for this position?

In this case, by asking the interviewer what they feel, you are setting them up to agree with you and give you more valuable information. This can be very effective, and be the cement that you are looking for.

If the interviewer has already supported your statement within the conversation (with a nod, verbal approval, or previously), your closing question will not be necessary. The answer that you give will be a reminder of their feelings, and as a bonus, it will show that you were listening!

NOW YOU TRY:

_____

_____

_____

_____

_____

_____

_____

QUESTION #9: *If you could describe yourself in 1 word, what would that word be?*

EXPLANATION: Believe it or not, I have seen people lose out on getting a job, even after having a strong interview, because they did not answer this correctly. Interviewers want to see if you can make a quick decision about who you are, and if you can follow directions.

SUGGESTON: The first thing that you want to do is to have a prepared answer. The interviewer wants the icing on the cake, not the whole cake. The word should enhance the qualities of everything that the interview has covered. If you cover a cake in dirt it may still be a delicious cake, but it will appear to be a pile of dirt. If you cover it with sweet frosting, you will get people dreaming about how good it will be.

More important, make this answer exactly ONE word. Multiple words show that you are not able to follow instructions. Not following instructions shows that you are a poor listener. This will ruin your credibility with the interviewer, because listening is the key to gaining instant respect.

Remember, until this point you have described yourself to the letter of what they are looking for. Now you want to say something that interviewers hardly hear:

Honest

Honesty is very important. Why should this person trust you? They should trust you, because you have done your research, supported your findings, and have showed them complete respect. Interviews are one of the quickest binding relationships that you will ever establish.

If you are in a relationship, when do you feel like it is time to make a commitment? The answer should be, when you have asked enough questions, and learned enough about the other person to be both happy and comfortable with them.

As long as you do not embellish or stretch the truth during the interview process, the person interviewing you will be very comfortable that you are an honest person.

NOW YOU TRY:

_____ (I still recommend the word "Honest" unless there is a key word that the interviewer keeps mentioning).

QUESTION #10: *Are there any other questions?*

EXPLANATION: This is the last question that we will be reviewing, and it is the most important question. If you have followed this system, and answered most of your questions with questions, then there is only one reason the interviewer is asking. They are inviting you to ask them for the job. If you don't then you lose out.

Consider yourself on a date. If you do not ask for a second date at the end of the first, then it looks like you are not interested. When you call in a few days, the person that you shared a tub of popcorn with is already dating your best friend. Always ask, then follow up.

SUGGESTION: On this question, make sure that you use your "Silent Umm" (pause for approximately three seconds) before answering. It will seem like an eternity, but you will have their undivided attention.

Look the interviewer directly in their eyes, and say the following:

Thank you for answering all of my questions completely. What is the next step within the hiring process?

Because you thanked them for answering your questions completely, they have no choice but to answer this one completely as well.

NOW YOU TRY:

_____
_____
_____
_____

■■■

There were ten questions within this section. There will be a lot more that you will encounter on various interviews. These however are the most commonly asked. If you can answer the ten questions with confidence, all of your other answers will come easy to you. Practice before each interview, and you will be able to get through it with great success.

GOOD LUCK & HAVE FUN!

CLUE#8

The end of your journey

MARKS THE SPOT!

You have reached clear, blue skies, and your goal is in sight. Use the tools that you have accumulated over your travels, and uncover your treasure. Do not let obstacles get in your way. You have both the strength and resources to dig past them.

Conclusion

What Has Been Uncovered?

When your journey began you were faced with a map that promised a treasure. This treasure was to be the career that you have always wanted. You were also told that if you followed each step completely the path would lead you directly towards your goal.

The purpose of this book was to help you to see your true value, and to learn how to find employment where others do not think to look. Each section that you have completed has shown you the right path, and even though you will be able to use this information to get the career that you deserve, the real treasure is...

Notes